30 Days to

A More Dynamic Prayer Life

JOHN FRANKLIN

30 Days to
A More Dynamic Prayer Life
Making God Your Focus

NAVPRESS

Discipleship Inside Out™

NavPress is the publishing ministry of The Navigators, an international Christian organization and leader in personal spiritual development. NavPress is committed to helping people grow spiritually and enjoy lives of meaning and hope through personal and group resources that are biblically rooted, culturally relevant, and highly practical.

For a free catalog go to www.NavPress.com
or call 1.800.366.7788 in the United States or 1.800.839.4769 in Canada.

NavPress titles may be purchased in bulk for ministry, educational, business, fund-raising, or sales promotional use. For information, please call NavPress Special Markets at 1.800.504.2924.

ISBN-13: 978-1-61521-881-3

Cover design by Arvid Wallen

Some of the anecdotal illustrations in this book are true to life and are included with the permission of the persons involved. All other illustrations are composites of real situations, and any resemblance to people living or dead is coincidental.

Unless otherwise identified, all Scripture quotations in this publication are taken from the New King James Version (NKJV). Copyright © 1982 by Thomas Nelson, Inc. Used by permission. All rights reserved. Other versions used include: the *Holy Bible, New International Version*® (NIV®), Copyright © 1973, 1978, 1984 by International Bible Society, used by permission of Zondervan, all rights reserved.

Printed in the United States of America

1 2 3 4 5 6 7 8 / 16 15 14 13 12

Pray!®

Deepening Your
Relationship with God
Through Prayer

Pray! resources from NavPress are for people who believe that talking with God was meant to be more than a predictable, duty-driven, one-way monologue. They're for people who want to pray with engagement, relationship, and life. They're for those of us who want to *experience* God and not just talk at Him.

If you're ready to break through obligation, guilt, boredom, and frustration into the relationship with God you've always wanted, *Pray!* books and resources are here to help.

Talking with God can be the satisfying connection your soul longs for. Are you ready to go deeper through prayer?

Contents

How to Use This Book

At the start of a new year, our family discussed what we hoped would happen by the end of it. My ten-year-old son piped up, "I want to know God better this year." You can imagine the joy that swelled within this father's heart, but his statement also stopped me dead in my tracks. There he stood on the precipice of the front end of his life, innocently looking ahead and expressing the desire for that which would have the single greatest impact on his time on Earth. The profundity of the moment, lost on him but fully obvious to me, flooded my mind with a host of swirling thoughts—most of them related to the implications of my responsibility as a father.

After my emotional dust settled, I reflected more on that moment. Being his father gave me a special interest in his request, but in reality his heart symbolized multitudes of Christians of all ages. He really wanted to know God. I've spoken to thousands of Christians around the country who voice a similar yearning. Sometimes, like my son, they state it as a matter of fact, sometimes with exuberance, but more often than not they do so with a disturbing hint of uneasy dissatisfaction with their Christian experience. They desire something more than what they've known. In varying degrees they cry out for God to become alive to them. They ask questions such as, "Why doesn't God seem more real to me?" "Why am I not experiencing abundant life?" "Is it possible to know God as people in the Bible knew Him?"

Perhaps you've chosen to use this book because you are someone who seeks a deeper walk with God. Scripture makes it explicitly clear that God desires to give you that very thing (see John 14:21; 17:26). He wants every one of His children to know Him in an ever-increasing manner, yet oddly enough, few Christians experience a consistent, victorious walk with God. That raises the question, "Why?" I am convinced one of the key problems stems from not knowing how to pray scripturally.

Consequently, Christians experience a pattern of wanting to do better, making a commitment to do so, failing to connect with God, losing interest, feeling guilty for losing interest, making a commitment to do better . . . and become stuck, repeating the cycle all over again.

This book is written to provide practical help in walking with God through understanding and practicing the basics required for dynamic prayer. Typically, there are three primary ways this book can be used: (1) individual study, (2) small-group study, (3) church-wide study. General guidelines for each method are provided below, while specific suggestions for individual or group study of each theme are provided in the free downloadable study guide at www.navpress.com/30days.

FOR INDIVIDUAL STUDY

The purpose of this book is to marry biblical teaching on prayer with practical application. Here are suggestions to help you get the most out of this material if you plan to do it on your own.

Set aside a place and a time to meet with God every morning for the next 30 days. Let me challenge you to zealously guard this time. Our schedules are extremely hectic, and things will happen along the way to derail you. Commit to a willingness to sacrifice in order to do whatever it takes to draw near to God. The effort will be well rewarded by knowing God better at the end of these 30 days.

Before you begin the prayer exercises, read the entire introduction so you can understand the goals of this book and how the book is structured to accomplish them.

Take note of the third section of each day, titled "Seek First the Kingdom." You will choose at least one prayer request to pray for consistently over the next 30 days. Focusing on one request creates a greater likelihood of learning how God responds to your prayers. Although this doesn't start until day 2, you may want to think about it ahead of time. A good prayer request to choose is something that's on your heart. This is a suggestion, not a rule. You may pick something else, but in Scripture, people prayed for and received answers for those things especially on their hearts. Watch for God's answers. Watch for insights from Scripture or prayer in your quiet time; watch for what happens in your world during the day that relates to your request.

There are seven themes found in the prayer exercises, and each theme will be covered in detail. When you complete the daily training exercises in each theme, consider referring to the study guide and completing the lesson related to each theme.

FOR SMALL-GROUP STUDY

This study works well in a group of about three to eight members who will meet for seven weeks. Each weekly session will last an hour. Suggestions for facilitating these sessions, including the introductory session, are provided in the study guide (free at www.navpress.com/30days).

FOR CHURCHWIDE STUDY

This book may be used as a discipleship tool for all or part of the church in at least five ways:

1. **Churchwide small groups.** You may organize multiple small groups to go through this study at a time that fits your church schedule. Possibilities would include Sunday school/Bible study, Sunday-evening discipleship, or home cell groups.
2. **Churchwide large group.** A pastor could lead the whole church through the study on Sunday mornings or evenings as a large group.
3. **Special emphasis.** This study could mobilize special prayer for an important upcoming event in the life of the church. For example, if the church is about to start a building campaign, a church plant, a new missions emphasis, and so on, the church could use the study course guide as a tool to pray for this over a six-week period.

4. **Leadership development.** The pastor could develop a prayer discipleship strategy by personally inviting key leaders to go through the book with him or her over a six-week period.

5. **Church development.** The same prayer discipleship strategy for leaders could be expanded to all adults. In a church of one hundred adult members, the pastor could easily disciple half the church in a year. In larger churches, staff or key leaders could mentor others.

Methods one, four, and five, in my opinion, are usually the best way to use the book. The study guide for churchwide use is the same as that for a small group and is available free at www.navpress.com/30days.

HOW THIS BOOK IS STRUCTURED

The structure of the book consists of three components. Knowing these components will familiarize you with what to expect in the pages ahead and help you understand their purpose.

1. Thirty daily training exercises. I've used the term *training exercise* rather than *devotional* because you will be putting into practice what you are learning about prayer. Each training exercise follows a format that guides you in praying. The purpose for 30 days of training exercises is to form the habit of daily prayer.

2. The format. The format of each training exercise is divided into five sections: Focus on God, Respond from the Heart, Seek First the Kingdom, Present Your Requests, and Close in Joy. The purpose of the format is to establish a consistent pattern for biblical prayer. It will focus your mind and heart on God in key ways.

3. Seven themes. The 30 training exercises are organized into seven themes: The Three Foundations of Prayer, God Trains You, Focus on God, Respond from the Heart, Seek First the Kingdom, Present Your Requests, and Close in Joy. The first two themes address truths for dynamic prayer. The last five explain the format we are using. You will see an explanation of the seven themes introduced before days 1, 4, 11,

14, 21, 29, and 30. These explanations list training goals for each theme to incorporate into your prayer life. The purpose of the themes is to highlight and focus your attention on what is important in the training exercises that will follow.

WHAT YOU WILL DO

1. Pray through the 30 training exercises. Depending on whether you are using this book individually or as a small group, you will set aside time each morning to spend with God over the next 30 days or 6 weeks. Each day you will read a training exercise that will guide your prayer time. Do not read more than one training exercise per day.

   2. Follow the format. The format of the training exercises follows biblical principles from the Lord's Prayer. Below I've briefly described the five sections and their purpose to clarify what you will do and why:

- **Focus on God**—Jesus taught us in the Lord's Prayer to begin prayer with "Our Father." Since you are in a relationship, you concentrate on the person of God before your needs. In this time you will focus your attention on Him in various ways, such as who He is, His attributes, His nature, His ways, His likes and dislikes, and His purposes.

- **Respond from the Heart**—As we focus on God, His Spirit reminds, encourages, corrects, strengthens, teaches, and guides us. Our job is to respond by worshipping, thanking, and praising Him and repenting of what does not conform to His image. Your mind will be renewed to serve Him willingly with joy whatever the circumstance or cost. Your love for God will grow.

- **Seek First the Kingdom**—In the Lord's Prayer, praying for His kingdom to come precedes asking for our daily bread. In healthy relationships both parties put each other's desires ahead of their own. God already knows the things we need before we ask (see Matthew 6:8). He promises that if we seek His interests first, He will add everything else to us (see Matthew 6:33). Therefore, we pray about God's concerns before we pray about personal concerns. God's kingdom desires are for His Son to be glorified, His church and individual Christians to be edified, the lost to be converted, and righteousness to increase in society.

- **Present Your Requests**—God is concerned about you. Scripture encourages us to cast all our cares on Him because He cares for us (see 1 Peter 5:7). You can pray about the things on your heart that personally impact you. Present to Him your needs, wants, wishes, and desires. In healthy relationships there is open communication by both parties.

- **Close in Joy**—Time with God can fill us with encouragement. The goal is not to manufacture an emotion, but if your mind has been renewed, then your attitude as you step out into the day can be filled with faith, joy, confidence, and so on—the fruit of the Spirit and a sense of abundant life in Christ. This short section of the format brings closure to time alone with God and transitions us to walk with Him during the day.

One final comment regarding the format—a relationship with God is not a formula. This format is simply a way to help you organize your mind, heart, and time in order to create a God-centered pattern of prayer in your life.

TWO KEYS TO DYNAMIC PRAYER

Have you ever tried to put a puzzle together without the picture on the box? Worse yet, have you ever tried with the wrong picture? Could you put together the pieces of a dynamic prayer life with no idea, or a mistaken idea, of what it looks like? Perhaps you would eventually, but you will greatly speed up the process by having a clear understanding of where you're going. In the remaining pages, I've written on two keys that create a box-top picture of what makes prayer dynamic. Incorporating these keys takes longer than a month, so don't strive for perfection. Strive for growth.

Sometimes to understand something you need to begin with what it is not. Prayer is not primarily about asking and receiving any more than a dog is primarily about barking. Suppose you bought a puppy and your whole understanding of how to raise a dog was limited to getting the puppy to start or stop barking. You would experience him responding in that way from time to time, but it would make your dog relationship grossly misguided. In the same way, if you approach prayer primarily as asking and receiving, that will make your relationship with God grossly misguided from what it ought to be.

By definition prayer is communication with God about everything involved in a relationship with Him. This includes knowing God, seeking first His kingdom, fulfilling His purpose on earth, asking and receiving resources to accomplish that purpose, interceding for others, becoming conformed to His image, and sharing your heart with Him— to name just a few. Therefore, to pray effectively you must know how a relationship with God works and the healthy patterns of communicating with Him. This book addresses both. If you are just learning to pray, I suspect you will be surprised by the next few pages. Paying attention to them, however, will greatly speed up your learning curve.

Key 1: Understand and Practice the Three Foundations

In my own life I have both succeeded and struggled in prayer. I can't think of a time that my successes or failures weren't caused by the presence or absence of these three foundations:

1. Practicing prayer as a relationship. God created you for relationship with Himself; therefore, the primary purpose of prayer is to know God intimately by experience. Those who sought God in Bible times and throughout history were marked by a passion, a hunger, a yearning for the person of God. For example, the apostle Paul declared, "What is more, I consider everything a loss compared to the surpassing greatness of knowing Christ Jesus my Lord, for whose sake I have lost all things. I consider them rubbish, that I may gain Christ" (Philippians 3:8, NIV). John Hyde, the great missionary nicknamed "Praying Hyde," spoke of sometimes being so enraptured in God he forgot to ask for anything. George Müller, who recorded over 50,000 answers to prayer in his lifetime, wrote that his most important business every morning was to get his soul in a happy state (delighted in God) before God. These men prayed because they longed for God, not from duty. They practiced prayer as a relationship, not a spiritual discipline. They desired *Him* more than what He gave.

This kind of relationship with God does not happen overnight. It deepens over time as we seek God and increasingly know Him by experience. Don't expect to start at the same place as these men who had walked with God for years. What I'm trying to establish is the standard. Your desire for relationship with God determines whether or not you'll walk with Him in prayer.

2. Praying consistently about your kingdom purpose. In Scripture, the moment God called people into relationship, He simultaneously gave them an assignment (see Genesis 2:15; Mark 1:17; 1 Peter 4:10). Then God began revealing Himself to them and through them as they were fulfilling His purpose. For example, in Acts the disciples prayed for and received the Holy Spirit to fulfill their assignment to be witnesses in Jerusalem, Judea, Samaria, and the ends of the earth. Peter and John prayed and were filled with the Spirit so they could proclaim Jesus boldly. Paul and Barnabas were called out during a prayer meeting to the work that the Spirit assigned them. This pattern makes sense. We are servants. Servants have an assignment. If we have an assignment, God will be talking to us about it and working through us to fulfill it. In the early stages of a Christian's life, that assignment usually is seemingly minor, such as helping at church or sharing your faith. How you respond in obedience will determine if your prayer life stays in fellowship with God. If you do not expect this as fundamental to a dynamic prayer life, you can become disoriented and wonder where God is. However, when you awake each morning and pray with a clear sense of God's kingdom purpose for your life, God will answer you powerfully and consistently.

3. Praying from a biblical mind-set. If you see horse manure, do you get excited that there's a horse nearby or become grumpy that you must clean up the mess? Your mind-set radically affects the joy you have in the Lord, what God grants you, and how He uses you for advancing His kingdom. For example, on the night Jesus was betrayed, He spoke to the disciples about His joy, asked the Father to do several things for the disciples, and was able to correctly handle the assignment of the Cross. Jesus' belief system, attitude, and focus resulted in His staying on track, the Father giving Him everything He asked for, and the salvation of the world. Likewise, you must train your mind to think biblically and discipline your attitudes according to the mind of Christ.

In my own life there have been three seasons in particular when I lacked the joy of the Lord. In each instance my mind-set was marked by patterns of worry or materialism. The dominant thoughts and attitudes of my life were contrary to Scripture. Returning to fellowship with God required a good deal of energy to discipline my mind-set. If you have never trained your mind to think biblically, you may find this practice will take time. However, as you increasingly think on and do what God instructs in His Word, you will find a growing depth of intimacy with Him.

Key 2: Understand That God Has Initiated a Training Process in Your Life Through Prayer

What do you expect to be different about your prayer life at the end of 30 days? What about 3 years? What about 30 years? Most people start prayer without an expectation beyond the here and now. But the eternal God views it quite differently. He sees what lies ahead, and He knows what He desires for your life. To accomplish His purposes, He initiates a training process so you become what He intends. That training finds us in one spiritual stage and transitions us to the next. The disciples' lives illustrate this truth.

Stage 1—In the Gospels, the power of God usually flowed minimally or inconsistently through the apostles' lives. They couldn't cast out the demon (see Mark 9:18); they wanted to call fire down on the offending Samaritans (see Luke 9:54); they requested the 5,000 go away (see Mark 6:36); they prohibited the children from coming (see Luke 18:15); they petitioned to sit on the right and left (see Mark 10:37); and so on.

Stage 2—In the book of Acts, however, Pentecost comes and 3,000 are converted (see 2:41); a man lame from birth is healed (see 3:7); the place is shaken (see 4:31); church conflict is resolved (see 5:5; 15:22); and so on.

God desires that we live stage-two book-of-Acts lives, rather than stage-one Gospels lives. Just as Jesus trained the disciples, so He desires to train us. Unfortunately, many Christians have no expectation that they must be trained; therefore, they neither look for nor participate with God in that process. Consequently, they try prayer, little happens, then they give up until the next need or crisis arises. In stage one God's primary goal is to train you in how to relate to Him for consistent fellowship and in His ways for the fulfilling of His kingdom purpose through you. He must teach and train you in several things, such as:

- What He is like—His character, ways, attributes, likes and dislikes
- The habits necessary to walk with Him consistently—Scripture reading, prayer, immediate obedience, denying self, faith, love, thanksgiving, becoming God-centered
- How to hear His voice—what it takes to get on praying ground, how to recognize when He is speaking, what creates an inability to hear Him

After we learn these lessons well enough, God works consistently through our lives to impact those around us. This does not imply we reach perfection, but we now know better what He is like so we ask more in line with His desires. The disciples rarely received what they asked for in the Gospels (stage one) because they didn't understand Jesus. In the book of Acts (stage two) they received what they asked for because their asking lined up with His desires, purposes, and character. Likewise you will find this to be increasingly true in your life. The longer and further you walk with God, the more you will see and receive.

I'm not saying God will do nothing in a stage-one prayer life, but you should not be discouraged if you don't see immediate, dramatic results. Rather you should spend the majority of your prayer time seeking to know God and trying to conform each prayer request to what He reveals about Himself and His kingdom. If He does nothing, use it as a learning opportunity and change what you request next time, until you understand what pleases God. Through this practice you will transition to a God-centered, stage-two prayer life.

You are now ready to begin your 30-day journey. My prayer for you is the same one the apostle Paul prayed for the Ephesians: "that the God of our Lord Jesus Christ, the Father of glory, may give to you the spirit of wisdom and revelation in the knowledge of Him" (Ephesians 1:17).

REVIEW
How This Book Is Structured:

- This book consists of 30 training exercises.
- The format of each training exercise is divided into five sections.
- The 30 training exercises are organized into seven themes.

What You Will Do:

- You will pray through the 30 training exercises.
- You will follow the format as a pattern for prayer.

Two Keys to Dynamic Prayer:

- Understand and practice three foundations required for dynamic prayer.
- Understand that God has initiated a training process to develop an ever-increasing kingdom significance to your life.

THE THREE FOUNDATIONS OF PRAYER

TRAINING GOALS FOR THIS THEME

1. Understand that the three foundations for dynamic prayer are: a growing relationship with God, fulfilling your kingdom purpose, and disciplining your mind-set to conform to Christ's.
2. Practice beginning prayer by focusing on God first.

IMPLICATIONS FOR PRAYER

1. The two most common subjects of your prayer life will be knowing God and asking for kingdom purposes.
2. Because you come to know God as you fulfill your kingdom purpose, carrying out your assignment directly affects the quality of your relationship with Him.
3. When we don't have a godly mind-set, we have trouble hearing God. Therefore, in our prayer life we must regularly read Scripture to train and renew our mind.

DAY 1

Knowing God Through Relationship
Foundation 1

Focus on God

Read John 17:24-26. In this passage, Jesus summarizes His final thoughts and desires before His death. What was the one thing Jesus said He would be doing in your life (see verse 26)?

He will be making God known to you. Stop. Let that sink in. God Himself wants you to know Him. He desires the kind of relationship with you where you increasingly know and experience Him from this day forward.

In light of this fact, how do you expect Him to act if you diligently seek Him?

How do you expect Him to act if you ever treat your relationship with Him casually?

Respond from the Heart

What is your response to the God who desires to make Himself known to you?

- ☐ Overwhelmed! I'm incredulous! What?! Me?!
- ☐ Praise and thanksgiving. I'm unspeakably grateful. God, there is no one like You.

☐ Repentance. In light of His goodness, I want to repent of anything displeasing to Him.

☐ Other:

Tell God your heart and mind right now based on this truth.

Seek First the Kingdom

The natural response to this kind of God is to want to please Him. A foundational way He commands us to do that is to seek first His kingdom. The kingdom of God primarily involves believers and lost people submitting to His rule and righteousness increasing in the land. Therefore, pray for:

Fellow believers:

A lost person:

Community, state, or nation:

Present Your Requests

God cares about you. What is on your heart? Be transparent with the Lord, telling Him your personal desires.

Close in Joy

Have your mind and heart been renewed as you've prayed? Thank God for these things as you step out to walk with Him in His world.

DAY 2

Knowing God Through Your Kingdom Purpose Foundation 2

Focus on God

Yesterday we established that God wants to make Himself known to you. Today we will answer the question "How do you expect Him to do that?"

Read Mark 1:17 and 3:14. Notice in both verses that Jesus called the disciples to Himself and simultaneously gave them an assignment in His kingdom. As they lived out His assignment, they came to know Him. For example, the disciples came to know God as provider when they went on a mission trip with no money (see Matthew 10:9-10). Likewise, in your life, God has designed that you know Him as you fulfill the kingdom purpose He has given you. This impacts your prayer life, because in prayer you and God will talk about your assignment. In prayer you learn your kingdom purpose on the front end of your walk with God. I struggled for six years in prayer before discovering this in Scripture.

Have you ever asked God about the assignment(s) He has for you? If you have never thought about it, or if you are unsure what your assignment might be, would you ask God to reveal it to you? Often He shows you by touching your heart with Scripture or opening opportunities to serve. Write down anything that comes to mind.

Respond from the Heart

Based on this pattern of Jesus and the disciples, how do you sense you need to respond to God?

☐ Praise. Father, thank You for the privilege of serving.
☐ Faith. Father, I don't understand. I have lots of questions, but I know You will show me my kingdom purpose.
☐ Repentance. Father, is that why You seem so distant?
☐ Other:

Seek First the Kingdom

You may want to choose one thing to pray for consistently during the next 29 days to increase your understanding of prayer by watching how God answers you. After you have prayed today, remember to look for how God responds to you.

Fellow believers:

A lost person:

Community, state, or nation:

Present Your Requests

Speak to God transparently regarding what is on your heart. Make requests for your personal desires.

Close in Joy

Have your mind and heart been renewed as you've prayed? In what ways are you grateful, confident, and expectant as you step out into the world today?

DAY 3

Knowing God Through His Mind-Set
Foundation 3

Focus on God

Read 1 Corinthians 2:16. According to Scripture, you have been given the mind of Christ. What a mind thinks or believes forms a person's attitudes and actions. Based on what you know of Jesus' attitudes and actions, can you list some of the ways His mind thought?

Read Mark 4:38-40. What was the contrast between His mind and the disciples' minds?

Jesus' mind was focused on God. How did that focus form His perspective, disposition, and behavior?

Read John 16:32, Luke 10:21, and Matthew 26:53. Look for three more examples of Jesus' perception and attitude. Where do you see that His mind gave Him faith in danger, joy in God's ways, and confidence in times of trial?

How did this impact the way He prayed?

God wants to fill you with the same mind-set as Jesus. His Spirit's assignment is to renew you in the spirit of your mind (see Ephesians 4:23). A corrupted mind-set, one that's negative, complaining, fearful, and so on, will greatly hinder effective prayer. All Christians must be renewed daily. How does God want to fill you with the mind of ChristUse this morning?

Respond from the Heart

What area of your mind does God need to renew today?

- ☐ Confidence instead of fear
- ☐ Faith instead of worry
- ☐ Thanksgiving instead of complaining
- ☐ Other:

Take time to respond to Him right now.

Seek First the Kingdom

Incorporate yesterday and today's truths as you begin praying for the kingdom. Be alert throughout the day for how God is answering you.

Fellow believers:

A lost person:

Community, state, or nation:

Present Your Requests

What personal concerns would you like to present to the Lord?

Close in Joy

How has your heart been prepared to walk with Him in your world today? Thank Him as you conclude your time of prayer.

GOD TRAINS YOU

TRAINING GOALS FOR THIS THEME

1. Have an expectation that God will be actively at work training you in how to have consistent fellowship with Him. Just as Jesus trained the disciples, so will He train you.

2. Have an understanding of what that training looks like.

3. Expect changes requiring your effort and sacrifice. You can have confidence that His training will result in your life being used for His purposes.

IMPLICATIONS FOR PRAYER

1. Prayer is about you listening to God more than Him listening to you.

2. It is important to practice what you are learning and sensing in your prayer time.

3. Seeking to understand God's ways (how He works) needs to be a significant priority.

4. Prayer isn't always warm and fuzzy but often requires a life response.

5. There will be a growing connection between your prayer time and your daily life.

DAY 4

God Trains You to Relate to Him

Focus on God

Read Mark 1:17 in one of the following translations: NASB, ESV, NKJV, or KJV. Did you notice that when Jesus called Peter and Andrew, He said, "Follow me and I will make you *become* fishers of men" (emphasis added)? In order for them to "become," Jesus had to train them. He had to lead them through numerous changes in their understanding of God, how they related to Him, and how they related to others before He could grant them significant kingdom responsibility in Acts. Likewise, God must train you before He can give you significant kingdom responsibility. That means your prayer life will include much listening and moving out of your comfort zone (not merely asking and receiving). That means daily God will actively be seeking to train you.

How do you recognize when God is training you? How do you respond to Him in the midst of the training process?

Respond from the Heart

Over the next few days we will explore what that training looks like and how to respond, but the first step begins with faith. We are to be filled with anticipation concerning what He has in store for us.

In light of this truth, how will you respond to God?

☐ Father, I thank You that just as You did not fail to train the disciples, neither will You fail to train me. I know You will make my life count.

☐ Father, I joyfully agree to cooperate with You in that process no matter what. I know it will pale in comparison to what You give in exchange.

☐ Father, I confess that I have been careless and not looking for You. I had no idea. From this day forward I want to be trained.

☐ Other:

Seek First the Kingdom

Pray for those on your heart. Watch for how God is answering you today.

Fellow believers:

A lost person:

Community, state, or nation:

Present Your Requests

What personal concerns would you like to present to the Lord?

Close in Joy

How has your heart been prepared to walk with Him in your world today? Thank Him as you finish your time of prayer.

DAY 5

God Trains You to Respond to His Authority

Focus on God

Very few people have accused the disciples of being exceptionally bright in the Gospels. Why then do you suppose Jesus chose them?

Read Mark 1:16-20 and John 6:60,66-68. What do you notice about the disciples?

The disciples may have been slow learners, but did you see how they recognized the authority of Jesus and obeyed Him immediately? Likewise, God has ordained that your training will depend not on your intelligence, but on your obedience. God will test and train you until you respond quickly and willingly. As you learn this habit, He will increasingly reveal Himself to you and use you for His glory. All training of our lives begins with this submission to God's authority.

Respond from the Heart

In light of this truth, how will you respond to God's authority over your life?

☐ Meditation. This is all new. Help me understand about Your authority.

☐ Thanksgiving. Father, I want to obey because I know You use Your authority wisely and consistently for my good and the good of others when I obey.

☐ Repentance. Father, I'm sorry I've been dragging my feet in obeying. I wasn't clueing in.

☐ Other:

Seek First the Kingdom

Pray for those on your heart. Watch for how God is answering you today.

Fellow believers:

A lost person:

Community, state, or nation:

Present Your Requests

What personal concerns would you like to present to the Lord?

Close in Joy

How has your heart been prepared to walk with Him in your world today? Thank Him as you conclude your time of prayer.

DAY 6

God Trains You to Be God-Centered

Focus on God

Read Matthew 16:21-23. Notice what transpired: Jesus revealed God's purpose of the Cross, Peter balked, and then Jesus corrected him. Pay special attention to how Jesus trained him: He immediately sought to transform Peter by identifying Peter's problem as a mind set on the things of man instead of the things of God. He sought to move him from being man-centered to God-centered.

This second way God trains us is to transform our mind from a self-centered orientation to a God-centered orientation. Jesus constantly teaches us who He is, what He is like, what His ways are, and the habits we need to remain God-centered. This happens intensely in the beginning of our walk with God and continues consistently throughout the remainder of our life.

Respond from the Heart

Below are practical questions designed to help you think about your God-centeredness. Take an inventory of how you spend your time each day.

As you reflect on a typical day, what seem to be your priorities?

How much time do you give to setting your mind on God—to intentionally praying and reading His Word?

Our minds are being influenced daily by politics, cultural values, entertainment, current events, trials, and so on. What does it take for your mind to be renewed each day from the messages that are contrary to Scripture?

To what degree do you exert yourself to put God's Word into practice after hearing sermons or reading Scripture? Is there any habit of forgetting and going about your business?

How do you need to respond to Jesus this morning? Do you sense He is calling you to make any lifestyle changes?

Seek First the Kingdom
Pray for those on your heart. Watch for how God is answering you today.

Fellow believers:

A lost person:

Community, state, or nation:

Present Your Requests
What personal concerns would you like to present to the Lord?

Close in Joy
How has your heart been prepared to walk with Him in your world today? Thank Him as you conclude your time of prayer.

DAY 7

God Trains You to Know His Love

Focus on God

The initial motivation for following God can arise from any number of reasons, but over time God particularly establishes one that supersedes all others.

Compare Luke 5:1-10 and John 21:1-19. At first, Peter's motive to follow sprang from the wonder of the miracle. The second time Jesus called Peter to follow from the motive of His love for him. The first time Peter didn't know Jesus. The second time he had experienced life with Him—days of working together, learning, sacrificing, sharing joys and sorrows. Likewise, in your relationship, God builds an understanding of His love for you through the experiences of life. Your ability to recognize God demonstrating His love to you will determine everything about the vibrancy of your prayer life. This third way God trains His children determines the long-term quality of your relationship with God.

Respond from the Heart

What is the quality of your love relationship with God? Is it vibrant, occasional, or something you have only read about in the Bible? Check which box describes your feelings:

☐ I've never experienced that. What would it look like?
☐ Yes, I regularly recognize and experience His love.
☐ No, but I would like to know Him that way.
☐ Sometimes I experience His love, but not often.
☐ Other:

Respond to God based on the box you checked.

Seek First the Kingdom

Pray for those on your heart. Watch for how God is answering you today.

Fellow believers:

A lost person:

Community, state, or nation:

Present Your Requests

What personal concerns would you like to present to the Lord?

Close in Joy

How has your heart been prepared to walk with Him in your world today? Thank Him as you conclude your time of prayer.

DAY 8

God Trains You to Hear His Voice

Focus on God

Read John 10:4,27. Any dynamic relationship requires communication. Notice that Jesus speaks to His sheep and they hear His voice. Would you not expect, then, that He speaks to all His children? If He didn't:

How could you experience His love?

How would you know where, when, and how to serve Him?

How could you respond to His training?

Therefore, God trains us to learn what His voice is like. In the beginning, we often don't know how to recognize God speaking to us (see, for example, 1 Samuel 3:1-10). As we seek Him through Bible study, prayer, and the counsel of other godly Christians, we become more familiar with His voice. As God continues to train us to hear Him and we obey, we receive more regular guidance from Him. This training is the normal way God deepens our love relationship, increases our joy, and develops our lives for increasing kingdom impact.

Respond from the Heart

How is God training and working with you right now?

☐ I don't have a clue how to hear God. Lord, please teach me!
☐ I know His voice, but sin has choked my ability to hear Him.
☐ I think I am hearing Him, but I'm not always sure.
☐ I hear God's voice and follow in obedience.
☐ Other:

Pray in response to God based on what you checked.

Seek First the Kingdom

Pray for those on your heart. Watch for how God is answering you today.

Fellow believers:

A lost person:

Community, state, or nation:

Present Your Requests
What personal concerns would you like to present to the Lord?

Close in Joy
How has your heart been prepared to walk with Him in your world today? Thank Him as you finish your time of prayer.

God Trains You to Put Off and Put On

Focus on God

Read the following passages and note the italicized words.

> Seek first the kingdom of God and His *righteousness,* and all these things shall be added to you. (Matthew 6:33, emphasis added)

> If I regard *iniquity* in my heart, the Lord will not hear [my prayer]. (Psalm 66:18, emphasis added)

> If any of you lacks wisdom, let him ask of God . . . and it will be given to him. But let him ask in faith, *with no doubting,* for he who doubts is like a wave of the sea. . . . Let not that man suppose that he will receive anything from the Lord. (James 1:5-7, emphasis added)

> That you *put off . . .* the old man which grows corrupt . . . and that you *put on* the new man which was created according to God, in true righteousness and holiness. (Ephesians 4:22,24, emphasis added)

What is common to these four passages?

Is it not that the cleanness of our heart determines whether or not God listens to us? Therefore, Jesus spent time constantly training and correcting the disciples' hearts. When they jockeyed for position, He urged them to put off pride and put on humility. When they viewed people as an annoyance, He told them to lay aside their perceptions and take up God's. When they couldn't cast out a demon, He exhorted them to exchange their unbelief for belief. According to 2 Peter 1:5, virtue and moral excellence precedes knowledge. Therefore, learning a lifestyle of continuous repentance is fundamental to prayer. God calls us to put off and put on.

Respond from the Heart

Conviction of sin is not to be feared or viewed as "God beating me up." When God leads us to put off and put on, there's nothing better for us than that. In light of God's goodness, how would you like to respond?

- ☐ Thank You, God, for conviction of sin.
- ☐ I want to repent of the sin of _____.
- ☐ God, what would You like me to put off? What would You like me to put on?
- ☐ Other:

Seek First the Kingdom

Pray for those on your heart. Watch for how God is answering you today.

Fellow believers:

A lost person:

Community, state, or nation:

Present Your Requests

What personal concerns would you like to present to the Lord?

Close in Joy

How has your heart been prepared to walk with Him in your world today? Thank Him as you conclude your time of prayer.

DAY 10

God Trains You to Respond in Faith

Focus on God

Read Mark 1:17. Do you remember this verse from day 4? We noted that Jesus promised the disciples, "Follow Me, and I will make you *become* fishers of men" (emphasis added). Fishers of men was the end result. Become was the process. In effect Jesus was saying, "If you spend the next three and a half years of your life with Me, I'll take you through a training process so that you'll become the kind of men through whom I will turn the world upside down." In the Gospels, the disciples usually missed it. In the book of Acts, they did indeed turn the world upside down.

How did Jesus transform them? What did He emphasize in His training?

Read Matthew 8:10, 9:22, and 15:28. What did Jesus always point out when He saw it?

Read Matthew 6:30, 8:26, 14:31, and 16:8. What did He always do when they failed to demonstrate faith?

Describe Jesus' view of faith.

Respond from the Heart

One reason faith is so important to God is because without it you can't be trained. You will have to trust Him as He leads you into difficult situations, allows trials, and assigns you "impossible" tasks. As you persevere, then you experience the mighty power of God working in you and through you to change your world.

How will you respond to God today?

Seek First the Kingdom

Pray for those on your heart. Watch for how God is answering you today.

Fellow believers:

A lost person:

Community, state, or nation:

Present Your Requests

What personal concerns would you like to present to the Lord?

Close in Joy

How has your heart been prepared to walk with Him in your world today? Thank Him as you finish your time of prayer.

FOCUS ON GOD

From this point forward, each theme will correspond to one of the five sections of the format. This theme corresponds to the section of the format titled "Focus on God."

TRAINING GOALS FOR THIS THEME

1. Understand that all extended times of prayer begin by focusing on God.
2. Learn how to do that practically.

IMPLICATIONS FOR PRAYER

1. If you train yourself to focus on God, you will be in position to recognize His voice.
2. If you don't begin prayer by focusing on God, you will rarely connect with Him.

DAY 11

Start with God, Not Your Request

Focus on God

One of the best ways to learn to pray is to watch how godly men and women did it in the Bible. Read Nehemiah 9. Note how much time passed before those praying asked for anything. Did you notice that they read the Book of the Law, confessed and worshipped half the day, then prayed for twenty-eight verses before making their request in verse 32? Why is this? They are becoming God-centered before making requests. When you enter an *extended* time of prayer, such as your morning quiet time or a prayer meeting, always begin with focusing on God. (In fact, every detailed record of a prayer meeting in Scripture follows this pattern. Not a single one *began* with praying for needs.) Three good reasons for this include:

1. Beginning extended prayer times by focusing on God trains us that He is the center of our lives and frees us from the tyranny of our needs that demand so much of our attention and attempt to control the agenda of our lives.
2. Beginning with God causes us to see from His viewpoint. In Nehemiah 9 they understood what to ask for because they understood their circumstances from God's perspective.
3. It is proper and fitting; He is the God of the universe, the Almighty, the Eternal One, the great King. He, His heart, and the things of His kingdom should receive attention first.

Therefore, in extended, set-aside times of prayer, you must begin with God.

Respond from the Heart

Had you heard the above truths before? This was the secret of the great prayer warriors of the Bible. Practicing them will bring a wonderful intimacy with God, allow you to be used by God, and set you free in ways you never dreamed possible.

Would you like to have this kind of relationship with God? How should you respond today?

☐ Father, would You please teach me how to focus on You?
☐ Father, would You cause me to hear what's on Your heart?
☐ Father, would You help me to see what You want me to see?
☐ Other:

Seek First the Kingdom

Pray for those on your heart. Watch for how God is answering you today.

Fellow believers:

A lost person:

Community, state, or nation:

Present Your Requests

What personal concerns would you like to present to the Lord?

Close in Joy

How has your heart been prepared to walk with Him in your world today? Thank Him as you conclude your time of prayer.

DAY 12

Focus on God Through the Renewing of Your Mind

Focus on God

On day 11, you read that all extended prayer times in the Bible begin by focusing on God, not presenting requests. Today we'll look at how God touches you to make that happen.

Read Romans 12:2 and Ephesians 4:23. Did you notice that you are renewed in your mind? Until that happens you will not connect with God in prayer. For example, in Matthew 20:17-21 Jesus clearly taught His disciples that He would be crucified. James and John responded to this earth-shattering revelation by asking to sit on His right and left. Why do you suppose they responded like this?

When they first realized Jesus was the Messiah, their minds immediately focused on how that impacted them rather than how they could serve Him. They responded from a mind set on their glory, ambitions, and honor instead of His. Until their focus changed they were of little use to God. They were still unprepared to assume leadership.

Respond from the Heart

Becoming God-oriented usually begins with renewing your mind and becomes completed when His truth sinks down into your heart.

What thoughts preoccupy your mind?

What are the desires of your heart?

To what extent are your thoughts and desires aligned with God's thoughts, His desires, His kingdom, and His work?

Spend time now turning your heart to Him. Ask Him to teach you how to renew your mind.

Seek First the Kingdom

Pray for those on your heart. Watch for how God is answering you today.

Fellow believers:

A lost person:

Community, state, or nation:

Present Your Requests

What personal concerns would you like to present to the Lord?

Close in Joy

How has your heart been prepared to walk with Him in your world today? Thank Him as you conclude your time of prayer.

DAY 13

Use the Bible Above All

Focus on God

Read Psalm 119:9,25,28,65,107,169. What phrase did you notice being repeated in these verses?

The Bible is the primary means God's Spirit uses to transform, shape, or renew our minds. Not surprisingly, about 10 percent of Jesus' recorded words were quotes or references from the Old Testament. In Acts the apostles' sermons and prayer meetings were filled with Scripture. Therefore, you should be regularly feeding on God's Word. You do this by meditating. Do not read Scripture like the newspaper, but carefully, slowly, asking questions all the while. As you read, ask the Holy Spirit to impact your understanding with a phrase, verse, passage, or pattern. This process focuses your mind on God and sensitizes you to do His will. Dwell on how you will respond to what God is showing you. This practice has helped my prayer life more than anything else I've done.

Respond from the Heart

Think about the verses you read today. How did they impact you?

What about other verses since you started this book?

What is God trying to say to you? How will you respond?

Seek First the Kingdom

Pray for those on your heart. Watch for how God is answering you today.

Fellow believers:

A lost person:

Community, state, or nation:

Present Your Requests

What personal concerns would you like to present to the Lord?

Close in Joy

How has your heart been prepared to walk with Him in your world today? Thank Him as you finish your time of prayer.

RESPOND FROM THE HEART

This theme corresponds to the section of the format titled "Respond from the Heart."

TRAINING GOALS FOR THIS THEME

1. Understand that your heart must respond to God in order to have fellowship with Him.
2. Practice basic ways your heart responds to God.

IMPLICATIONS FOR PRAYER

1. Reading Scripture will be of no benefit without a heart response to what God shows you.
2. A heart response requires mind, will, and behavioral changes, not only being emotionally stirred.
3. Failure to adjust your life indicates you have not yet adjusted your heart.

DAY 14

Your Heart Must Respond

Focus on God

Read Jeremiah 29:13, Matthew 5:8 and 13:14-15, and Hebrews 10:22. What do these verses have in common?

Did you recognize a pattern? God has ordained that we find, see, hear, and draw near to Him according to the condition of our heart. The heart makes up the totality of a person's being. It determines our loyalty, values, passions, love, will, thinking, and mind. When God speaks, we must adjust our heart to match His. In short, we must respond. Prayer that ceases responding to God, ceases encountering God. Many people have difficulty in prayer because they grow casual about diligently responding to God. They mistakenly equate being stirred emotionally as the biblical definition of a correct heart response.

Respond from the Heart

Read the following questions. Use them to guide your prayer time.

Do you love the Lord as much today as you ever have?

How are you maintaining passion for God, service to Him, and the determination to do His will?

In what ways are you (or could you be) exercising godliness?

What do you need to put into practice?

Seek First the Kingdom
Pray for those on your heart. Watch for how God is answering you today.

Fellow believers:

A lost person:

Community, state, or nation:

Present Your Requests
What personal concerns would you like to present to the Lord?

Close in Joy

How has your heart been prepared to walk with Him in your world today? Thank Him as you close your time of prayer.

DAY 15

Praise and Thanksgiving

Focus on God

Read Psalm 100. Thanksgiving and praise are usually involved in beginning an extended prayer time. To praise and thank God are some of the most common commands connected to prayer. Many good reasons exist why this is true. Here are four:

1. Thanksgiving and praise turn our eyes from self and circumstances onto God.
2. We become like what we praise. We imitate what we admire (see 2 Corinthians 3:18).
3. How could we not? Could we respond any other way to the One who has redeemed us; has given us His Son, eternal life, and the privilege to reign with Him; and will withhold nothing else from us?
4. Thanksgiving and praise are two of the indispensable heart practices that nurture love. Romans 1:21 reveals that the first step in a heart turning away from God is the failure to glorify (praise is involved in glorifying) and thank Him.

Thanksgiving is responding in gratitude for what God has done for us. Praise is responding to who God is.

Respond from the Heart

Make a list of what God has done for you and the people you care about. Make another list of His attributes (for example, holiness, nobility, love, mercy, and so on).

Spend time thanking and praising Him based on your list.

As a way of expressing your gratitude to God, would you be willing to let go of any grumbling and complaining as you walk with Him today?

Seek First the Kingdom

Pray for those on your heart. Watch for how God is answering you today.

Fellow believers:

A lost person:

Community, state, or nation:

Present Your Requests
What personal concerns would you like to present to the Lord?

Close in Joy
How has your heart been prepared to walk with Him in your world today? Thank Him as you conclude your time of prayer.

Love for God

Focus on God

Read Psalm 31:23. As David meditated on what God had done for him, what was his reaction? David loved God and wanted everyone else to love Him as well! When we focus on who God is and what He has done for us, love is a natural heart response. Our love for God increases as we perceive His love for us. When we see what He has done for us, we desire to give to Him, serve Him willingly, and put His agenda ahead of our own. When Christians do not practice focusing on the person of God, they usually struggle to find intimacy with Him. They may become duty driven, listless in passion, or perhaps legalistic. Their love for God will often grow anemic. God desires the kind of relationship with us that is marked by authentic love for Him, love that grows continually stronger and deeper.

Respond from the Heart

God wants to bring all His children into a deepening love relationship with Himself.

Describe how you are learning to recognize and experience His love for you.

What have you sensed Him doing in your life recently to show His love to you?

Is there anything that hinders your love for God?

Spend time now responding to God.

Seek First the Kingdom

Pray for those on your heart. Watch for how God is answering you today.

Fellow believers:

A lost person:

Community, state, or nation:

Present Your Requests

What personal concerns would you like to present to the Lord?

Close in Joy

How has your heart been prepared to walk with Him in your world today? Thank Him as you close your time of prayer.

DAY 17

Worship

Focus on God

Read Psalm 95:6. Many churches today might define worship as adoration. While adoration is an aspect of worship, it's wholly inadequate as a root definition. In the Bible the root concept of worship in both Hebrew (*shachah*) and Greek (*proskeneo*) is the idea of submission or bowing down. Worship is primarily the heart response of submission in recognition of God's preeminence. The most common relationship pictured in Scripture between the one worshipping and the One worshipped is servant to Lord (see Joshua 5:14). When I recognize His greatness, I willingly submit my life or possessions to His will. Therefore, biblical worship is fundamentally marked by a lifestyle of service to God (see Romans 12:1, NIV, NASB). If we become emotional on Sunday morning but our lifestyle fails to change, we have not biblically worshipped. However, when we focus on God and see Him as He is, not only does our heart adore Him but we joyfully submit our lives in service to Him for His glory.

Respond from the Heart

With the above definition of worship in mind, how does your worship affect your daily lifestyle?

What changes have you made as a result of being in God's presence?

Think of the worthiness of God to receive power, riches, wisdom, blessing, strength, honor, and glory (see Revelation 5:12) — not to mention your possessions and very life. Is there any "Isaac" (see Genesis 22 — an "Isaac" is something dear to you) in your life that you need to lay on the altar? If so, what is it?

How and what should you submit to Him as "your spiritual act of worship" (Romans 12:1, NIV)?

   If you are physically able, consider praying on your knees today as an expression of worship.

Seek First the Kingdom

Pray for those on your heart. Watch for how God is answering you today.

Fellow believers:

A lost person:

Community, state, or nation:

Present Your Requests
What personal concerns would you like to present to the Lord?

Close in Joy
How has your heart been prepared to walk with Him in your world today? Thank Him as you conclude your time of prayer.

Repentance

Focus on God

Read Isaiah 6:1-5. Did you notice that when Isaiah saw God, he immediately recognized his sin? He instantly saw the discrepancy between himself and God. Likewise, as we focus on God, we will see areas in our lives that do not match the character of Jesus. When we perceive this, the natural response is to repent.

Repentance does not mean merely feeling sorry for sin but turning from it. It is a way I worship God — by allowing His Spirit to conform me into the image of Christ. He does that by taking Scripture and bringing to my attention areas of my life that need changing. When He does this, He is not condemning me or beating me up, but rather expressing His love to me. If He were to leave me alone, I would experience the consequences of what the sin would eventually produce. If I refuse to confess my sin, I will not see God nor will He listen to me when I pray (see Matthew 5:8; Hebrews 12:14; Psalm 66:18).

Respond from the Heart

A good way to let God search your heart is to examine regularly whether your life matches Scripture. Read Ephesians 4:29–5:4. As you read each verse, confess and repent of any sin God surfaces.

4:29—Has any corrupt word proceeded from your mouth recently?

4:31—Have you been putting away bitterness, wrath, and anger?

4:32—Are you forgiving others as God forgave you?

5:2—Are you walking in love?

5:3—Is there any sexual immorality or greed in your life?

5:4—Do you constantly give thanks?

Seek First the Kingdom

Pray for those on your heart. Watch for how God is answering you today.

Fellow believers:

A lost person:

Community, state, or nation:

Present Your Requests

What personal concerns would you like to present to the Lord?

Close in Joy

How has your heart been prepared to walk with Him in your world today? Thank Him as you finish your time of prayer.

DAY 19

Faith

Focus on God

Hebrews 11:6 says, "Without faith it is impossible to please [God]." Does that mean God is grieved if you pray without expectation or confidence in Him?

The answer is *yes*. The verse goes on to say that anyone "who comes to God must believe that He is, and that He is a rewarder of those who diligently seek Him." This means you can be sure that when you bow before your God, He will respond to you. Not one single time did Jesus fail to answer any request the disciples made of Him. Sometimes the answer was no, sometimes yes, sometimes He simply taught them—but He always answered. It ought to never enter your mind that God is not going to respond to you, unless you have sin you are clinging to (see Psalm 66:18; Matthew 5:24) or you doubt that He will (see James 1:5-8). You can pray with faith and expect a response from Him.

Respond from the Heart

Is your heart ready this morning? Do you really expect God to answer you?

☐ Yes
☐ No
☐ Not sure

Prepare your heart to pray in faith for the requests you are going to bring before God. Remember faith is not determining what the answer will be, but confidence that God will respond to you. Start praying today when you are confident God will respond to you.

Seek First the Kingdom

Pray for those on your heart. Watch for how God is answering you today.

Fellow believers:

A lost person:

Community, state, or nation:

Present Your Requests

What personal concerns would you like to present to the Lord?

Close in Joy

How has your heart been prepared to walk with Him in your world today? Thank Him as you close your time of prayer.

DAY 20

Resolve

Focus on God

Read Matthew 26:39-44. Why do you think Jesus had to pray three times about the Cross?

What do you think He meant by His admonition to the disciples in verse 41?

How have you experienced the truth of what Jesus says in the second part of verse 42?

How do feelings, fears, fatigue, and desires impact our actions?

Jesus' warning clearly shows that oftentimes we want to obey God, but if we don't steel our hearts with resolve, we won't carry through when pressures come. Jesus set the example of continuing in prayer until He was resolved to walk with His Father no matter what. By having His mind and heart renewed, Jesus was strengthened with unshakable determination to carry out God's will. Our resolve to do God's will and to resist temptation must be nourished each day. This generally happens when the joy of the Lord is the source that strengthens our resolve (see Nehemiah 8:10). The joy of the Lord is more than emotion—it is the delight of knowing God and what He's done. This joy is usually renewed as we feed on His goodness, faithfulness, promises, and actions toward us.

Respond from the Heart

How has God been working on your resolve to do His will no matter what?

What are some areas in which He has been strengthening you, or that He wants to strengthen?

☐ Removing strongholds
☐ Perseverance
☐ Speaking up
☐ Obedience
☐ Other:

Spend time meditating on God's goodness to you and what He has in store through your obedience. Thank and praise God until your heart genuinely desires to do His will today.

Seek First the Kingdom

Pray for those on your heart. Watch for how God is answering you today.

Fellow believers:

A lost person:

Community, state, or nation:

Present Your Requests

What personal concerns would you like to present to the Lord?

Close in Joy

How has your heart been prepared to walk with Him in your world today? Thank Him as you conclude your time of prayer.

THEME 5

SEEK FIRST THE KINGDOM

This theme corresponds to the section of the format titled "Seek First the Kingdom."

TRAINING GOALS FOR THIS THEME
1. Understand what the kingdom is.
2. Understand that God grants your personal needs if you put His kingdom first.
3. Practice praying for God's interests first, before praying for your interests.

IMPLICATIONS FOR PRAYER
1. If you want to see God's power, you must seek His kingdom first.
2. Your whole life needs to be increasingly bent toward fulfilling your kingdom purpose(s) in life.
3. Your kingdom purpose(s) starts with edifying fellow believers. If you are faithful in a little, you will be given greater responsibility.

DAY 21

What Seeking the Kingdom Means

Focus on God

Read Matthew 6:10,13,33. Did you know that Jesus mentioned the kingdom of God more than He did heaven, hell, and eternal life combined? The condition He put on receiving things from God was whether or not we seek first His kingdom. That means it would be rather important to know what the kingdom is and how to seek it!

What do you think it means to seek the kingdom of God?

The kingdom is wherever the rule and reign of the King are present. Seeking the kingdom means you take action for the things to come about on earth that increase it. The main components of the kingdom are:

- The glorification of Jesus
- The edification of God's people
- The conversion of the lost and an increase in societal impact

Over the next few days we'll look at each one of these.

Respond from the Heart

In what ways do you seek God's kingdom first?

Do you sense any area you would like to change in order to make seeking God's kingdom more of a priority?

Would you ask God to tell you at least one thing you could do today to seek His kingdom? Write down what you think He might be saying.

Do not be surprised if an idea comes to mind while you pray in the section below. Be ready to respond.

Seek First the Kingdom

Pray for those on your heart. Watch for how God is answering you today.

Fellow believers:

A lost person:

Community, state, or nation:

Present Your Requests

What personal concerns would you like to present to the Lord?

Close in Joy

How has your heart been prepared to walk with Him in your world today? Thank Him as you conclude your time of prayer.

DAY 22

Pray for the Father and Son to Be Glorified

Focus on God

Read John 14:13 and Matthew 6:13. Did you notice that in John 14:13 Jesus connects the promise to do what we ask to the condition of whether it glorifies the Father? In the Lord's Prayer in Matthew 6:13, Jesus teaches that the whole direction of our praying ought to be linked to advancing the kingdom and God's glory. These are related. When God is glorified, His reign in human hearts increases, resulting in Christians serving Him all the more and the lost being converted. When this happens, the kingdom comes "on earth as it is in heaven" (Matthew 6:10). Therefore, in seeking first the kingdom, our prayers will include seeking God's glory. Many people's prayers center on themselves instead of God being glorified; therefore, they rarely experience God responding to their prayers. Those whose prayers seek God's glory experience Him responding powerfully.

Respond from the Heart

How have you been living to glorify God? Here are questions for meditation:

What could you pray for that would result in God being glorified?

How does seeking God's glory change your prayers?

Does anything come to mind about how you could decrease in order that Jesus might increase (see John 3:30)?

Do not be surprised if an idea comes to mind as you pray in the section below.

Seek First the Kingdom

Pray for those on your heart. Watch for how God is answering you today.

Fellow believers:

A lost person:

Community, state, or nation:

Present Your Requests

What personal concerns would you like to present to the Lord?

Close in Joy

How has your heart been prepared to walk with Him in your world today? Thank Him as you close your time of prayer.

DAY 23

Pray for the Church to Be Edified

Focus on God

Read Ephesians 4:12,16,29. Did you notice that the function of every part of the body is to build or edify other members? Jesus is intensely concerned that the whole body and each individual member come to maturity, that we use our gifts, resources, and mouths to build others up according to their need, not to tear them down. Therefore, our prayers for others will include requests for building them up. After we pray, we look for opportunities God creates to meet others' needs and then take advantage of them. When those we pray for and serve are strengthened, then they have greater love, endurance, and zeal to serve the Lord. In this manner the body is built up, which results in His kingdom advancing more and more.

Respond from the Heart

As we mature, the Holy Spirit often leads us to evaluate our prayer life. We may ask questions such as "How am I praying for fellow believers to be strengthened in their relationships with God?" "Is the orientation of my life to think about my needs or others' first?" How would you like God to grow your prayers for others?

When you pray for someone, God often involves you in becoming the answer to your request. What opportunities for involvement is God creating for you?

Thank God for the privilege of praying for your brothers and sisters in Christ. Thank Him in the confidence that He will respond to you on behalf of those you are about to intercede for.

Seek First the Kingdom
Pray for those on your heart. Watch for how God is answering you today.

Fellow believers:

A lost person:

Community, state, or nation:

Present Your Requests
What personal concerns would you like to present to the Lord?

Close in Joy
How has your heart been prepared to walk with Him in your world today? Thank Him as you finish your time of prayer.

DAY 24

Pray for the Lost and Societal Impact

Focus on God

Read 1 Timothy 2:1-4. Verse 4 states that God desires all men to be saved; therefore, we should pray for the lost. Did you notice that Paul connects praying for kings and those in authority as having a direct impact on people being saved? When a community, state, or nation's rulers uphold standards of morality, the people under their rule increase in their understanding of right and wrong. When people understand right and wrong, they more readily realize they are accountable and thereby more readily fear God. When they fear God, they more readily repent. Therefore it is important to pray for our leaders so that the lost may be converted and righteousness may increase in the land.

Respond from the Heart

How is God growing your prayer life to include the lost? Is it broader than just the Christian friends you know?

Think of your local community leaders, governor, and president. In what ways might God be leading you to pray for them?

As you talk to God in the next section, make sure to include key leaders in your prayers for your community, state, or nation.

Seek First the Kingdom
Pray for those on your heart. Watch for how God is answering you today.

Fellow believers:

A lost person:

Community, state, or nation:

Present Your Requests
What personal concerns would you like to present to the Lord?

Close in Joy
How has your heart been prepared to walk with Him in your world today? Thank Him as you conclude your time of prayer.

DAY 25

Recognizing and Responding to God's Activity

Focus on God

Read Acts 10:17,19,34. Notice that the revelation of God's will was a process requiring Peter's response along the way. Though God could have explained everything all at once, He chose to make it clear as Peter walked in obedience one step at a time. The same will be true in your life. Do not pray and expect God always to make His will clear from beginning to end. Do not pray and expect God to answer you without your involvement. Recognizing and responding to God each step along the way will determine whether or not your prayer request is granted in the majority of cases. This is when prayer becomes really exciting and moves from praying a list to experiencing God in your life. If you don't know how to walk with God this way, do not be troubled. The process requires time and effort, but God will teach you as you diligently seek Him.

Respond from the Heart

How does the above paragraph strike you?

☐ Come on, God doesn't speak or guide people today like He did in the Bible.

☐ I don't know how to do that, but I'm excited and grateful that He's already in the process of training me.

☐ Yes, I've experienced Him doing that and know how to walk with God that way.

☐ Other:

Take time with God now, asking Him to help you recognize and respond to His guidance for the things that you are praying.

Seek First the Kingdom

Pray for those on your heart. Watch for how God is answering you today.

Fellow believers:

A lost person:

Community, state, or nation:

Present Your Requests

What personal concerns would you like to present to the Lord?

Close in Joy

How has your heart been prepared to walk with Him in your world today? Thank Him as you close your time of prayer.

DAY 26

Recognizing and Responding to God's Activity from Scripture

Focus on God

God wrote Scripture as an infallible record of His character, purposes, and ways. It establishes the standard for discerning who God is, what He intends, and how He goes about it. A thorough biblical education orients us to God so that when He does something in or around our lives, we recognize Him and know how to respond. Therefore, Scripture is the foundational means the Holy Spirit uses in sensitizing us to Him. How does He do it?

Read Psalm 51:6. Did you notice what God desires and where He desires it? When you understand Scripture or are impacted by it in your inmost being, that is God speaking to you. He speaks to let you know something about His relationship with you or how He is inviting you to follow Him; therefore, when you are being impacted by Scripture, you should ask, "God, why are You touching my heart or understanding in this manner? What are You telling me? How do You want me to respond?"

Respond from the Heart

What Scriptures has God been bringing to your heart lately?

How are these Scriptures connected to what you have been praying?

How might He be trying to communicate something that goes beyond any specific request you've been asking?

Take a moment to meditate on verses or passages that have impacted you lately. What is God saying?

Seek First the Kingdom

Pray for those on your heart. Watch for how God is answering you today.

Fellow believers:

A lost person:

Community, state, or nation:

Present Your Requests

What personal concerns would you like to present to the Lord?

Close in Joy

How has your heart been prepared to walk with Him in your world today? Thank Him as you finish your time of prayer.

Recognizing and Responding to God's Activity Among His People

Focus on God

Read Philippians 1:6 and 2:13. God is always working in His people. The key is to recognize Him so that you will know how to pray and respond in line with His activity. There are at least four ways that you may recognize God working in someone:

1. When that person has a hunger for God and spiritual things. The desire for God, to study the Bible, to have a deeper prayer life, to become more like Jesus, and so on, only comes from God.
2. When that person desires to serve and sacrifice for Christ. Satan does not urge people to serve in the things of God or to put others first.
3. When that person is seeking ways to build up others. When God's people desire to minister to one another, meet each other's needs, and build unity and fellowship, God is motivating them.
4. When a Christian demonstrates strength in trial. The ability to face cancer, job loss, death of a loved one, or some other trial with unusual strength comes from God.

When we see God's activity in others, we should pray about how we are to respond.

Respond from the Heart

How is God working in your church?

As you observe His work, how does it direct your praying?

Is there any response to take in light of what you are seeing?

Praise and thank Him now for what He is doing.

Seek First the Kingdom

Pray for those on your heart. Watch for how God is answering you today.

Fellow believers:

A lost person:

Community, state, or nation:

Present Your Requests

What personal concerns would you like to present to the Lord?

Close in Joy

How has your heart been prepared to walk with Him in your world today? Thank Him as you conclude your time of prayer.

DAY 28

Recognizing and Responding to God's Activity in Our World

Focus on God

Read Jeremiah 9:24. Based on this verse, where does God work? Depending on your translation (other than the New Living Translation), it probably reads "in the earth" or "on earth." That means God is always working out the three qualities of lovingkindness, justice, and righteousness in our world. How then would you recognize Him? Anytime one or more of the following happens in someone's life, community, state, or nation, it is God at work:

- Lovingkindness/faithfulness—God shows love and loyalty to those who are His own. He provides for them or comes through in their hour of need. Additionally, when you see an unbeliever asking spiritual questions, that is God demonstrating His love by drawing that individual to Himself (see John 6:44).
- Justice/judgment—God is the one who judges sin and rectifies injustice in the earth. He does that in order to teach righteousness to the inhabitants of the earth (see Isaiah 26:9).
- Righteousness—God works out circumstances for individuals and nations to help them know and do what is right.

When you recognize God working, that is an opportunity for you to respond.

Respond from the Heart

In light of the scriptural pattern of how God works, do you recognize anyone in your life whom He is working in?

Are you ready to pray for that person with expectation and joy?

How can you respond?

Seek First the Kingdom

Pray for those on your heart. Watch for how God is answering you today.

Fellow believers:

A lost person:

Community, state, or nation:

Present Your Requests

What personal concerns would you like to present to the Lord?

Close in Joy

How has your heart been prepared to walk with Him in your world today? Thank Him as you close your time of prayer.

PRESENT YOUR REQUESTS

This theme corresponds to the section of the format titled "Present Your Requests."

TRAINING GOALS FOR THIS THEME

1. Develop freedom and confidence to tell God anything on your heart.
2. Pray for personal concerns.

IMPLICATIONS FOR PRAYER

1. God wants you to tell Him what's on your heart.
2. You should never be intimidated to approach Him—not by failure, fear, or discouragement—not even by sin if your heart is contrite.

Presenting Your Personal Requests

Focus on God

Read Philippians 4:6-7 and 1 Peter 5:7. God and His kingdom are the dominant subjects of our prayers; however, God also cares deeply about us. In healthy relationships both individuals enjoy freedom to express anything that is on their hearts. God cares about you apart from your service to Him. He wants you to tell Him your greatest concerns. He grants you the freedom to be transparent before Him. Therefore, He urges you to entrust Him with all the things that are important to you—your dreams, aspirations, needs, heartaches, fears—everything!

Respond from the Heart

How much freedom do you sense in your relationship with God? How confident are you that you can trust Him with the deepest part of your heart?

Does anything hinder you from being completely transparent with God or wanting to pray? If so, tell Him about it and ask Him to help you.

How are you learning to cast your cares upon Him (without grumbling and complaining) with the confidence that He hears and will answer you?

If you don't have this kind of relationship with God, ask Him for it. Approach Him with an unclouded confidence that He cares for you and will answer you.

Seek First the Kingdom

Pray for those on your heart. Watch for how God is answering you today.

Fellow believers:

A lost person:

Community, state, or nation:

Present Your Requests

What personal concerns would you like to present to the Lord?

Close in Joy

How has your heart been prepared to walk with Him in your world today? Thank Him as you conclude your time of prayer.

CLOSE IN JOY

This theme corresponds to the section of the format titled "Close in Joy."

TRAINING GOAL FOR THIS THEME

1. Conclude your daily prayer time with a heart attitude that's ready to walk with God in His world.

IMPLICATIONS FOR PRAYER

1. Your morning prayer time does not end when you say "Amen." It prepares you to walk with God and seek His kingdom throughout the day with joy.

Leaving Your Prayer Closet

Focus on God

Read Acts 2:42,46-47. Did you notice that gladness and simplicity of heart were staples of the early Christians' walk with God? In the book of Psalms alone, the word *rejoice* occurs in forty-six verses, *glad* in twenty-two verses, *joy* in twenty verses, *delight* in nineteen verses, and the other words *rejoices, rejoicing, joyful, gladness*, and *celebrate* account for thirty more verses.

Our prayers lead us to remember the privileges we have in a relationship with God, renew the desire to deny self, see His kingdom come, and cast our cares on Him. Such prayers most often produce joy. The majority of healthy prayer times will result in rejoicing in God—not by ignoring trials or denying problems but by finding joy in the person of God. It is common to conclude a time of prayer in a spirit of celebration, anticipation, joy, or gratitude because we have been in God's presence.

Once your mind and heart are renewed, you now leave your prayer closet to serve Him in His world. Your communion with God doesn't end when you finish your prayer time; rather, it prepares you to walk with Him throughout the day, leading you or involving you in His work in the world.

Respond from the Heart

The way you close prayer can vary. It may be by singing a song, thanking God for what He said or did in your prayer time, or simply saying "Amen." The point is that your heart should be ready to serve God joyfully today. Do you have that attitude right now? How would you like to respond to God?

☐ Thank You that You will develop me into this kind of person.

☐ I'm there. I'm ready to enjoy and serve You today.

☐ I still have a way to go, God, but I know You are helping me to experience more of Your love and freedom, so I'm going to keep trusting You.

☐ Other:

Seek First the Kingdom

Pray for those on your heart. Watch for how God is answering you today.

Fellow believers:

A lost person:

Community, state, or nation:

Present Your Requests

What personal concerns would you like to present to the Lord?

Close in Joy

How has your heart been prepared to walk with Him in your world today? Thank Him as you close your time of prayer.

Final Thoughts

Congratulations! You have completed the 30 training exercises. I hope they encouraged you in your walk with the Lord. Sometimes when learning something new and seeing how far we have to go, we can actually become discouraged. Sometimes when things don't come quickly or easily, we find ourselves tempted to think, *What's the use?* My prayer for you is that this may not be the case, keeping in mind that Rome wasn't built in a day. We are all in process. These simple training exercises were meant to start you on the journey of a deepening prayer life and give you markers of what to look for and do along the way. May your relationship with God deepen, may your walk with Him sweeten, and may your usefulness for the kingdom ever increase.

May God's grace be upon you!

John Franklin

About the Author

JOHN FRANKLIN is a nationally known speaker in the area of prayer and spiritual awakening. His passion is to provide conferences and resources to arouse God's people to seek Him for personal and national revival. He has previously served as a prayer specialist for LifeWay Christian Resources; as minister of prayer at First Baptist Church of Woodstock, Georgia; and in two pastorates. Other books authored or coauthored by John are *And the Place Was Shaken: How to Lead a Powerful Prayer Meeting*, *Spiritual Warfare: Biblical Truth for Victory*, *By Faith: Living in the Certainty of God's Reality*, and *A House of Prayer: Prayer Ministries in Your Church*.

John is married to his wonderful wife, Kathy, and together they have three equally wonderful children, Daniel, Nathan, and Susanna.

Learn more about John and his ministry or contact him about speaking engagements by visiting www.johnfranklinministries.org.

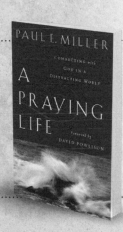

The *Message* Means Understanding

Bringing the Bible to all ages

*T*he *Message* is written in contemporary language that is much like talking with a good friend. When paired with your favorite Bible study, *The Message* will deliver a reading experience that is reliable, energetic, and amazingly fresh.

NAVESSENTIALS

Voices of The Navigators—Past, Present, and Future

NAVESSENTIALS offer core Navigator messages from such authors as Jim Downing, LeRoy Eims, Mike Treneer, and more — at an affordable price. This new series will deeply influence generations in the movement of discipleship. Learn from the old and new messages of The Navigators how powerful and transformational the life of a disciple truly is.

Meditation
by Jim Downing
9781615217250 | $5.00

Advancing the Gospel
by Mike Treneer
9781617471575 | $5.00

Laboring in the Harvest
by LeRoy Eims with Randy Eims
9781615216406 | $10.99

To order, go to **www.NavPress.com** or call **1-800-366-7788**.

SUPPORT THE MINISTRY OF THE NAVIGATORS

The Navigators' calling is to advance the gospel of Jesus and His kingdom into the nations through spiritual generations of laborers living and discipling among the lost.

Navigators have invested their lives in people for more than 75 years, coming alongside them life on life to help them passionately know Christ and to make Him known.

The U.S. Navigators' ministry touches lives in varied settings, including college campuses, military bases, downtown offices, urban neighborhoods, prisons, and youth camps.

Dedicated to helping people navigate spiritually, The Navigators aims to make a permanent difference in the lives of people around the world. The Navigators helps its communities of friends to follow Christ passionately and equip them effectively to go out and do the same.

To learn more about donating to The Navigators' ministry, go to **www.navigators.org/us/support** or call toll-free at **1-866-568-7827**.